Lewis & Clark

A Photographic Journey

Bill and Jan Moeller

Mountain Press Publishing Company
Missoula, Montana
1999

Second Printing, May 2000

Library of Congress Cataloging-in-Publications Data
Moeller, Bill, 1930–
    Lewis & Clark : a photographic journey / Bill and Jan Moeller.
      p.   cm.
  Includes bibliographical references and index.
  ISBN 0-87842-405-9 (alk. paper)
  1. Lewis and Clark Expedition (1804–1806) Pictorial works.
2. West (U.S.)—Discovery and exploration—Pictorial works. 3. West
(U.S.)—Description and travel. 4. Lewis, Meriwether, 1774–1809
Quotations. 5. Clark, William, 1770–1838 Quotations. I. Moeller,
Jan, 1930   . II. Title. III. Title: Lewis and Clark.
F592.7.M64   1999
917.804'2—dc21   99-34862
                                             CIP

PRINTED IN HONG KONG BY MANTEC PRODUCTION COMPANY

Mountain Press Publishing Company
P.O. Box 2399 • Missoula, MT 59806
(406) 728-1900

For Greg, Denise, and Eric

Contents

Acknowledgments

During our careers, we have written many books and have found that compiling a book that is mainly photographic is quite different from compiling a book that is mainly text. In addition to the writing, we must travel to the locations where we shoot the pictures. Often we need help in pinpointing or gaining access to these locations.

We are most grateful to those who have helped us in this regard: Chan and Kalley Biggs, Bureau of Land Management, Fort Benton, Montana; Tim Crawford, Gates of the Mountains Boat Tours, Helena, Montana; Bill Lutz, National Park Service, Knife River Indian Villages National Historic Site, Stanton, North Dakota; Ricardo Perez, Fort Clatsop National Memorial, Astoria, Oregon; Paul J. Pence, U.S. Army Corps of Engineers, Fort Peck, Montana; Lyle and Betty Lind, Fort Mandan, Washburn, North Dakota; Ron Williams, Lewis and Clark State Park, Onawa, Iowa; Kay Kreder, Lewis and Clark Center, St. Charles, Missouri; and Louis A. Clark of Wathena, Kansas.

Our thanks also to those at Mountain Press involved with the book, especially Gwen McKenna, our editor, and Kim Ericsson, who was responsible for the layout and design.

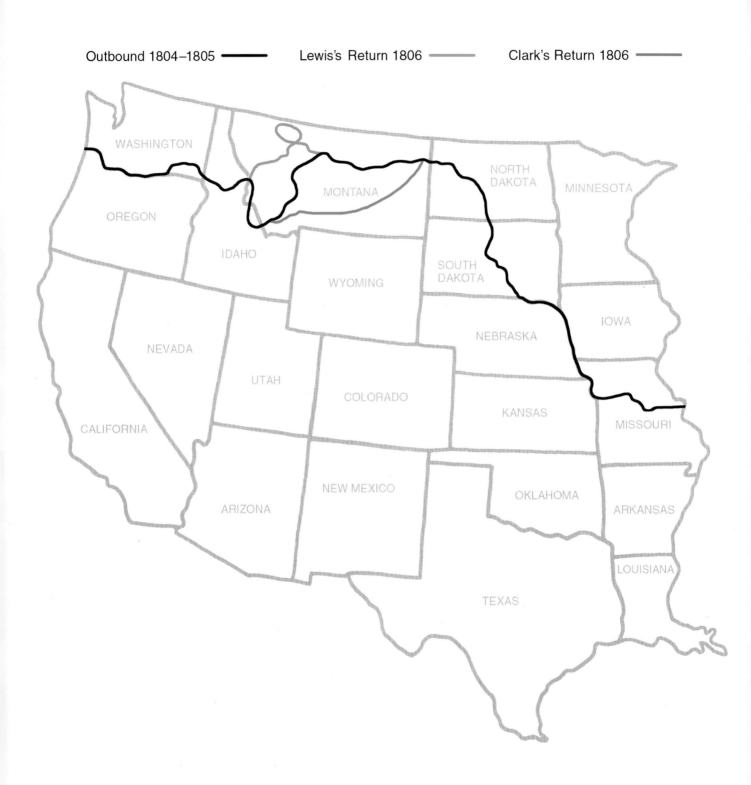

Outbound 1804–1805 ▬▬▬ Lewis's Return 1806 ▬▬▬ Clark's Return 1806 ▬▬▬

WASHINGTON

OREGON

MONTANA

IDAHO

NORTH DAKOTA

MINNESOTA

WYOMING

SOUTH DAKOTA

NEVADA

UTAH

COLORADO

NEBRASKA

IOWA

CALIFORNIA

KANSAS

MISSOURI

ARIZONA

NEW MEXICO

OKLAHOMA

ARKANSAS

LOUISIANA

TEXAS

Notes to the Reader

A traveler can explore the entire route covered by Lewis and Clark by automobile, except for the Missouri Breaks section. This section of the Missouri, designated as a Wild and Scenic River, can be explored only by boat. Also, although it's possible to drive over portions of the Lolo Trail, the road is isolated and rough; you should not attempt to drive it unless your vehicle is suited for this and you have the necessary equipment for such a trip.

Some information about disparities in spellings and place names: The spellings of the names of certain Indian tribes varies, depending on the source consulted. In all instances, the spellings we use are those most commonly in use today. The journals of Lewis and Clark are rife with misspellings. In most instances we have corrected the spelling in the quotes used. In keeping with today's usage, no apostrophes are used in geographic locations with possessive proper names, such as Marias River, but the apostrophes do appear in direct quotes from the journals. The captions on the photographs are the present-day names of the places shown.

Chapter 1
The Lure of the West

What do the vast lands of the West look like? What wonders do they hold? Who and what inhabit them? Might there be a northwest passage to the Pacific Ocean? These were questions to which President Thomas Jefferson wanted answers.

From boyhood, Jefferson had been fascinated by the West and its mysteries, and in 1802, two years after he was elected president, he was in a position to have his curiosity satisfied. He envisioned sending an expedition to explore the northern interior of the continent as far west as the Pacific Ocean. Never mind that the United States didn't own the territory. Originally owned by Spain, the area known as the Louisiana Territory had recently been ceded to France, though it remained under Spanish administration.

Jefferson approached the Spanish ambassador, Marques de Casa Yrujo, with his proposal to explore the territory. But Yrujo was coldly unreceptive to the plan, and he warned Jefferson that he would notify the Spanish government should the president try to pursue the idea. Jefferson, however, was not dissuaded. Unknown to Yrujo, he had already gotten an estimate of the cost of such an exploration—$2,500—and he had submitted his proposal to Congress. In his presentation to Congress, Jefferson pointed out that such an exploration could have significant trade benefits for the United States. In early 1803, Congress allocated the funds.

The Birth of the Expedition

To lead the expedition, Jefferson selected his personal secretary, Meriwether Lewis. The twenty-nine-year-old Lewis was delighted to accept the challenging position. Because of his military service on the western frontier, Lewis was well qualified for the job. As a captain he was

experienced in command, and during his service he'd had some dealings with Indians and had become acclimated to the rugged life and hardships of the frontier.

In March 1803, one of the first things Lewis did in planning the journey was to enlist the services of Lieutenant William Clark, with whom he had served on the frontier. Clark, with his similar military and frontier experience, was just the sort of person Lewis wanted as co-commander

William Clark. Portrait by Charles Willson Peale, circa 1810
—INDEPENDENCE NATIONAL HISTORICAL PARK

Meriwether Lewis. Portrait by Charles Willson Peale, circa 1807
—INDEPENDENCE NATIONAL HISTORICAL PARK

of the expedition. From his residence in Indiana Territory, the thirty-three-year-old Clark wrote to Lewis accepting the offer.

Lewis was to be in charge of collecting information pertaining to the natural sciences, and to prepare he went to Philadelphia to receive instruction from scientists at the University of Pennsylvania. Clark's duties would be those of engineer and geographer. Although both men had experience in river navigation, Lewis recognized that Clark was the better qualified in this area, so the two agreed that Clark would be responsible for managing the boats.

While plans for the expedition proceeded, Jefferson's special envoy, James Monroe, and the United States ambassador to France, Robert Livingston, were in France negotiating with Napoleon Bonaparte's representatives to purchase the French-owned New Orleans and West Florida. The two Americans were nonplussed when the French negotiators offered to sell the entire Louisiana Territory. The proposal was made because Napoleon's treasury was depleted and he needed funds for his military operations. Without authority to proceed, the two Americans decided to seize the extraordinary opportunity. For $15 million they

"The Signing of the Treaty," Jefferson City, Missouri

purchased all the French land between the Mississippi River and the Rocky Mountains, more than doubling the size of the United States.

Jefferson heard about the purchase six weeks later—just days before Lewis left Washington to begin recruiting men and securing supplies for the expedition. Now

LOUISIANA
PURCHASE
1803

that the land belonged to the United States, Jefferson could legitimately and openly go forward with his plans for the exploration of the West.

The northwest coast of North America had already been explored by a few mariners. One of them, Robert Gray, discovered the river he named after his ship, the *Columbia*, in 1791. For decades, fur traders and trappers had been plying the waters of the Missouri River well into what is now the state of North Dakota, a few venturing as far west as the confluence of the Yellowstone and Missouri Rivers. But what lay between the confluence and the Pacific coast was a mystery. No white men had ever seen it. This was the territory Lewis and Clark were to explore.

In a directive to Lewis, Jefferson set out the objectives for the journey: "The object of your mission is to explore the Missouri River, and such principal stream of it, as, by its course and communication with the waters of the Pacific Ocean, may offer the most direct and practicable water communication across the continent, for the purposes of commerce." Jefferson especially wanted to know whether any other western rivers were navigable, and whether the rivers could provide a better way of shipping furs from the Northwest than the present method, which entailed transporting the furs by ship via the long and perilous route around Cape Horn to East Coast ports. The president further instructed that latitudes and longitudes were to be recorded along the way, as well as information about the climatic conditions, soil types, vegetation, animals, minerals, and anything else deemed pertinent.

Jefferson also charged Lewis with obtaining extensive information about all the Indian tribes he encountered: their habits, clothing, dwellings, occupations, tools, and religion. The president stressed that Lewis and his men always "treat them in the most friendly and conciliatory manner which their own conduct will admit. Allay all jealousies as to the object of your journey, satisfy them of its innocence, make them acquainted with the position, extent, character, peaceable and

4

commercial dispositions of the U.S., of our wish to be neighborly, friendly and useful to them, and of our dispositions to a commercial intercourse with them."

Preparations for the Journey

On July 5, 1803, Lewis departed from Washington to make preliminary arrangements for the expedition. He spent six weeks in Pittsburgh—far longer than he had intended—waiting for the boatbuilder to finish the shallow-draft keelboat he had ordered weeks before. The boat was fifty-five feet long and had an eight-foot beam with oarlocks along each side. The thirty-two-foot mast could carry a large square sail as well as a foresail. Its cargo capacity was ten tons.

Keelboat replica, Lewis and Clark State Park, Onawa, Iowa

Reconstruction of 1740 courthouse, Cahokia, Illinois

A mere three hours after the boat was finished, Lewis had his supplies loaded aboard, and he and his crew set off down the Ohio River in company with a pirogue (a canoelike boat hollowed from the trunk of a tree). Downriver in Wheeling, West Virginia, Lewis purchased an additional pirogue. After negotiating the Falls of the Ohio, the flotilla put in at Clarksville, in Indiana Territory, to pick up Clark and his slave, Ben York. Here nine men were inducted into the army, making them the first permanent members of the Corps of Discovery—the name Jefferson had given

to the expedition. While the Corps would gain and lose a few members in these early stages, the inducted men were not free to come and go as they pleased.

More than a month later, Lewis stopped at the town of Cahokia, on the east side of the Mississippi, almost across from St. Louis. After picking up John Hay, the Cahokia postmaster, who spoke French, and Nicholas Jarrot, a French fur trader, Lewis crossed the river to St. Louis to meet with Colonel Carlos Dehault Delassus, lieutenant governor of Upper Louisiana, hoping to secure his permission to travel up the Missouri River. Lewis explained his purpose to Delassus, producing a letter from Jefferson as credential. The governor suggested that Lewis and his men wait in Cahokia until spring, because by then Upper Louisiana would belong to the United States.

Having been beset by delays from the start, Lewis knew that his original goal—to be about 300 miles up the Missouri before winter set in—was already impossible, so he agreed to wait. Hay recommended Wood River as a suitable place for a camp. Being only eighteen miles north of St. Louis, it would be convenient for obtaining supplies. It was also close to their departure point at the mouth of the

Missouri. The Corps arrived at the campsite on December 12, 1803.

That winter was a busy time; preparing for the expedition was no small undertaking. Supplies had to be obtained, catalogued, and packed; guns installed on the three boats; and personnel recruited and trained. But by spring, everything was finally ready for the voyage into the wilderness.

Vicinity of camp on Wood River, Wood River, Illinois

Chapter 2
Upriver to the Mandan Settlements

May 14—15, 1804

The Corps of Discovery, including Meriwether Lewis's Newfoundland dog, Seaman, departed from the Wood River camp. Most of the men were in the heavily laden keelboat and the rest in the two pirogues. They crossed the Mississippi River and proceeded upriver on the Missouri.

Shortly after setting out, the Corps encountered a good sampling of the river hazards that would be with them for many hundreds of miles: swift current, sandbars, eroding banks that sometimes carried trees with them, logs floating just below the surface of the water, and, perhaps most dangerous of all, sawyers—large tree trunks with one end anchored in the riverbed and the other springing up and down in the current, sometimes visible, sometimes not.

8

Mouth of Wood River, Wood River, Illinois

May 14, 1804, Monday

I set out at 4 o'clock P.M., *in the presence of many of the neighboring inhabitants. . . .*

(Clark)

May 16, 1804, Wednesday

We arrived at St. Charles at 12 o'clock. A number [of] spectators, French and Indians, flocked to the bank to see the party.

— (Clark)

May 16–21, 1804

After arriving at St. Charles, Missouri, the captains spent the ensuing five days securing additional supplies and recruiting a few more men, bringing their complement at that point to about forty-eight.

Missouri River, St. Charles, Missouri

May 22—June 9, 1804

The country the men first passed through resembled the eastern states from which they had come: riverbank timbered with hardwoods and familiar wildflowers in bloom. But within a few days the scenery gave way to tall limestone bluffs. Shortly after they left the bluffs region, they arrived at Arrow Rock, a location well known to both river and overland travelers.

Limestone bluffs on lower Missouri River

May 22, 1804, Tuesday

. . . some high lands on the starboard side.

(Clark)

June 9, 1804, Saturday

Several small channels running out of the river below a bluff and prairie (called the Prairie of Arrows) where the river is confined within the width of 300 yards.

— *(Clark)*

Arrow Rock vicinity, near Arrow Rock, Missouri

Missouri River
at Stump Island Park,
Glasgow, Missouri

June 10, 1804,
Sunday

Passed a large
island called
Chicot [a French
name meaning
stump].

——— (Clark)

The country about this place is beautiful, on the river rich and timbered. . . .

(Clark)

Missouri River from Fort Osage, Sibley, Missouri

June 10—23, 1804

First passing through more flat land, they entered a section with low bluffs on one side. Nothing remarkable, except for an island covered with stumps and a bluff that Clark thought would be an excellent location for a fort. (Indeed, he returned to the site in 1808 and supervised the building of Fort Osage.)

June 26, 1804, Tuesday

Passed a bad sand bar where our tow rope broke twice and with great exertions we rowed round it and came to and camped in the point above the Kansas River.

— (Clark)

June 24—July 4, 1804

After a few more uneventful days, the Corps reached the mouth of the Kansas, the first major river emptying into the Missouri. Until now, the Missouri had trended in a westerly direction, but now it made a broad sweep to the north. They camped here before moving upriver. On the Fourth of July they arrived at a small stream, which in honor of the day they named Independence Creek. The crew held a celebration that included firing the keelboat's swivel gun and enjoying the gill of whiskey the captains had issued for each man.

July 4, 1804, Wednesday

We . . . camped . . . above the mouth of a creek . . . we call Creek Independence. We closed the day by a discharge from our bow piece [and an additional] gill of whiskey [for the men].

— (Clark)

Missouri River at the mouth of the Kansas River, Kansas City, Missouri

Independence Creek, Atchison, Kansas

July 5—21, 1804

The Corps expected to encounter some Indians at the mouth of the Platte River, where they had hoped to begin fulfilling Jefferson's directive to assemble information on the various tribes. But, as Clark noted, because members of the Pawnee and Oto tribes "were out in the prairies following and hunting the buffalo, I fear we will not see them." He was right.

July 14, 1804, Saturday

The storm . . . struck our boat . . . and would have thrown her up on the sand island dashed to pieces in an instant, had not the party leaped out . . . and kept her off. . . . The storm suddenly ceased and the river became instantaneously smooth as glass.

(Clark)

Missouri River, Brownsville, Nebraska

Platte River near its mouth, Plattsmouth, Nebraska

July 21, 1804, Saturday

Arrived at the mouth of the Great River Platte. . . .
The current of this river comes with great velocity
rolling its sands into the Missouri. . . . We found great
difficulty in passing around the sand at the mouth. . . .

(Clark)

July 22—August 3, 1804

As the expedition moved farther upriver, they sent out messengers at each stop to try to contact the Indians. After several days, a trader named Mr. Fairfong, along with a party of Missouri and Oto Indians, came into the explorers' camp. The next day, after a parade of the Corps in their full-dress uniforms, both parties made speeches and smoked the peace pipe, and the captains presented gifts to the Indians. For gifts and trading, Lewis and Clark had brought a supply of needles, fishhooks, awls, and scissors, among other useful items; an assortment of beads and ribbon; vermilion paint; tobacco; and silver and copper medals to present to the chiefs.

August 1, 1804, Wednesday

Our camp is . . . covered with grass interspersed with copse of hazel, plums, currants, raspberries, and grapes of different kinds. The Indians not yet arrived.

— (Clark)

Fort Atkinson State Historical Park, Fort Calhoun, Nebraska

Missouri River below Sioux City, Iowa

August 4—16, 1804

The Corps moved on, hoping to meet members of the Omaha tribe, but they could find none. On the way, they stopped to visit the grave of the Omaha chief Blackbird, who in 1802 had succumbed to smallpox, along with many other Omaha. The grave was on a high knoll overlooking the Missouri.

August 17—20, 1804

There was still no sign of the Omaha. Three chiefs of the Oto came into camp hoping that Lewis and Clark could intercede for them to make peace with the Omaha, with whom they had been at war; however, this could not be accomplished because the Omaha were off hunting.

Sergeant Floyd is taken very bad all at once with a bilious colic. . . . He gets worse and we are much alarmed at his situation.

— (Clark)

On August 18, the Corps celebrated Lewis's thirtieth birthday, but any lingering gaiety of the occasion was offset when Sergeant Charles Floyd fell ill the next day. Clark ministered to Floyd as best he could, but at about noon the following day, as the Corps was moving upriver, Floyd died, probably of a ruptured appendix. The captains selected a nearby high bluff for his burial, which Lewis conducted with full military honors.

Monument on Sergeant Floyd's grave, Sioux City, Iowa

Buffalo

August 21—25, 1804

At the Corp's recent meeting with the Oto, the Indians had told a tale of eighteen-inch-tall devils inhabiting a hill farther north. At first the captains discounted the story, but then they decided that if the story were true, it would be better to investigate rather than leave the dis-covery to others. They found no devils, but upon reaching the top of the hill, the party was rewarded with a sweeping panorama of the plains countryside and, according to Clark, "numerous herds of buffalo were seen feeding in various directions."

August 25, 1804, Saturday

The only remarkable characteristic of this hill . . . is that it is insulated or separated a considerable distance from any other.

— (Clark)

Spirit Mound near Yankton, South Dakota

August 26—September 1, 1804

The expedition reached the mouth of the James River and set up camp at the base of a bluff. Here they had their first encounter with members of the Sioux tribe, the friendly Yankton.

Lewis and Clark held a council with members of the tribe, at which they and the Indians made speeches and the captains distributed gifts. Lewis and Clark persuaded the Yankton to agree to make peace with their neighbors. But one chief warned the white men that "those nations above will not open their ears," meaning that the aggressive Teton Sioux, farther north, would not be so amenable to the explorers and their suggestions.

August 28, 1804, Tuesday
We came to below the Calumet Bluff and formed a camp in the beautiful plain near the foot of the high land. . . .

— (Clark)

Calumet Bluff, Gavins Point Dam, Yankton, South Dakota

Mouth of the Niobrara River, Niobrara State Park, Niobrara, Nebraska

September 4, 1804, Monday ——————

This river widens above its mouth and is divided by sands and islands . . . not navigable for even canoes.

(Clark)

September 2—22, 1804

The landscape had gradually been changing, and now the explorers were truly on the high plains, an arid region where the abundance of trees gave way to vast, undulating expanses of prairie grasses. Wildlife was plentiful. The men saw some animals that were familiar to them, including many types of birds, elk, buffalo, and wolves, and others that were new to them, such as antelope, coyotes, prairie dogs, and deer larger than their eastern counterparts.

September 17, 1804, Sunday

. . . antelopes which we saw . . . feeding on the hills and plains.

(Lewis)

Antelope

29

September 23–28, 1804

The captains, upon learning of two Teton villages a few miles up the Bad River, a tributary of the Missouri, sent messengers ahead to request a council with the chiefs. The chiefs agreed to the meeting. Well aware that the Teton may be hostile, the explorers took the precaution of anchoring the keelboat midriver and leaving several of the expedition's men aboard.

September 23, 1804, Sunday

The river is nearly straight for a great distance, wide and shoal.

— (Clark)

Missouri River near Pierre, South Dakota

Mouth of the Bad [Teton] River, Fort Pierre, South Dakota

September 24, 1804, Monday

The tribe of the Sioux called the Teton is camped two miles up on the northwest side and we shall call the river after that nation, Teton. This river is seventy yards wide at the mouth of water, and has a considerable current.

(Clark)

The chiefs arrived on September 25. Both factions were on their guard, and the situation was tense. Communication was hampered because no one in the Corps knew much of the Sioux language. The Teton managed to make it known that they intended to control all trade goods in the area. They indicated that they wanted the power to keep or trade goods as they wished and to deny goods to their enemies, and they expected Lewis and Clark to help them. If their demand was not granted, they would take one of the pirogues and its cargo. Lewis and Clark made it clear that neither option was acceptable.

The captains' resolution was tested several times during the council. At one point there was a standoff in which the warriors made ready to shoot arrows and the explorers faced them down with rifles and the keelboat's swivel gun. No shooting from either side occurred, and tensions had eased somewhat by evening.

The chiefs wanted their women and children to see the boats, so the next day the boats were taken up the Bad River (Lewis and Clark named it the Teton) to one of the villages. The captains were treated as honored guests and smoked the peace pipe with the chiefs.

The captains returned to their boats to sleep, and the next night, September 27, two chiefs and another Teton stayed on board with them. In the middle of the night, the anchor cable parted when someone accidentally steered a pirogue into it. As the men scrambled to keep the boat from being swept away, the resulting noise alarmed the chiefs. One of them shouted that they were under attack by the Omaha. Within minutes the bank was lined with Teton warriors. The chiefs calmed down when they realized it was a false alarm. Nevertheless, a party of Teton remained, watching, on the bank for the remainder of the night.

Afterward, of necessity the keelboat was moored to the bank, and Clark noted in his journal: "All prepared on board for anything which might happen. We kept a strong guard all night in the boat, no sleep." The next day, after a fruitless search for the anchor, the explorers set off upriver, but not before another incident occurred: as the boat was being cast off, the Teton tried, unsuccessfully, to hold on to the mooring cable.

On-a-Slant Mandan village, Fort Abraham Lincoln State Historic Site, Mandan, North Dakota

September 29—October 19, 1804

Summer gave way to autumn, and the Corps was exposed to north winds, gray days, and frosty nights. No matter what the weather, they had to press on in order to find a suitable place for their winter quarters.

On October 8, the explorers came to the first of three Arikara villages in the vicinity, and within a week they had visited all three, holding councils and distributing gifts. The Arikara were much more amicable than the Teton. Lewis and Clark scouted the area looking for a likely place for their winter camp, but found nothing satisfactory.

October 20, 1804, Saturday

Camped . . . immediately above the old village of the Mandans.

(Clark)

October 26, 1804, Friday

We . . . camped . . . about a half mile below the first Mandan town.

— (Clark)

October 20—November 1, 1804

On October 20, the expedition camped near a deserted Mandan village. This tribe, who had been driven out by the Sioux, was now settled about sixty miles north on the Knife River. The first snow fell on October 24. Several parties of Mandan rode to the riverbank and followed the progress of the boats. One evening a party visited the explorers' camp.

Within a few days, the Corps reached the new Mandan settlement. Lewis and Clark spent many days meeting with the chiefs, distributing gifts, enjoying entertainments, and scouting out a location for the expedition's winter quarters because the captains had decided to winter here, near this friendly tribe.

Chapter 3
Winter at Fort Mandan

Soon after Clark located a suitable site, construction of a fort began. The Corps built the fort on the east bank of the Missouri, about three miles downriver from the nearest village. Fort Mandan, as they called it, was triangular, with an eighteen-foot-tall palisade forming each side. Along each side of the triangle were four rooms, each with a sleeping loft. The entry gate, at the base of the triangle, faced the river.

The weather was far from ideal during the construction. It was cold—cold enough for ice to begin forming on the river—and it snowed frequently. Although the fort was not yet completed, the men moved into it on November 20.

Fort Mandan reconstruction, Washburn, North Dakota

Earth lodge, Knife River Villages National Historic Site, Stanton, North Dakota

The Missouri was completely frozen over by early December, and the men were already experiencing the bitter cold that was to be with them until February. There were forty days during that period when temperatures never crept above zero. On the coldest day, the temperature was forty-five degrees below zero in the morning and by afternoon had risen to only twenty-eight degrees below.

On December 25, the Corps celebrated not only Christmas but also the completion of the fort. In honor of the occasion, each man fired one round of the swivel gun. A ration of rum was followed by a dinner of the best food in their stores.

Interior of an earth lodge, Knife River Villages National Historic Site, Stanton, North Dakota

Afterward they danced and frolicked throughout the evening.

The winter was filled with activities. When it wasn't too cold, the men went out in hunting parties. Traders for the North West and Hudson's Bay Companies were frequent visitors, coming from their post on the Assiniboine River in Canada, about a nine-day journey north. In addition, Lewis and Clark held numerous councils with the Mandan, Minitari, Sioux, and Arikara to try to persuade them to stop warring with one another.

Even more important were the sessions in which the Indians gave the explorers a wealth of information about the rivers and lands to the west, as far away as the Continental Divide. Most of the information came from the Minitari, who had ventured much farther west than the Mandan. Much of the Indians' information would prove to be quite accurate, but some of it was so wrong that it later led to confusion.

The five earth-lodge villages of the Mandan and Minitari had a combined population of about 4,400. There were some white men and their families living in the villages. Lewis and Clark hired one of them, a French Canadian fur trader named Toussaint Charbonneau, as an interpreter for the expedition. Charbonneau's Shoshoni wife, Sacagawea, and their infant son, Jean Baptiste, born on February 11, would also accompany the expedition, going at least as far as the lands inhabited by the Shoshoni in the distant west. Sacagawea had been living in the Minitari village since 1800, when she was captured by a Minitari war party that had invaded Shoshoni lands.

In March, when the weather began to warm, the Corps began constructing six more pirogues. They would need the smaller boats because the keelboat was too large to be used on the river above the villages. By March 25, the ice had begun to break up, and two weeks later, on April 7, 1805, the keelboat was sent back to St. Louis with a crew of eleven. Its cargo, a variety of plant and animal specimens, Indian artifacts, journals, maps of the explored area, and Lewis's detailed study of the Indians they had encountered so far, was to be delivered to Jefferson. That same afternoon, Lewis and Clark, with a company of thirty-three in the eight pirogues, set off into the unknown western territory.

Sculpture of Sacagawea and her son, Jean Baptiste, Bismarck, North Dakota

Chapter 4
Onward to the Coast

April 8—24, 1805

The explorers set out toward their next major objective—reaching the confluence of the Yellowstone and Missouri Rivers. As they proceeded upriver, they saw migrating geese, budding trees, and flowers that were beginning to bloom.

The weather was still cold, however, and several times severe winds caused problems for the expedition. Once, a sudden squall nearly overturned a pirogue, and on another occasion, high winds forced the party to lay over for a day. Provisions and supplies were subject to damage from the spray, and some days the wind blew so hard that the crew made little progress, even using the towropes.

To the delight of the captains, they found that the maps Clark had drawn from information provided by the Indians were accurate so far. The Little Missouri and the White Earth Rivers appeared where the Indians had said they would be. By now the explorers often saw grizzly bears in the distance, as well as grizzly tracks at the river's edge.

April 25, 1805

Here Lewis went on ahead, becoming the first of the party to see the Yellowstone River. He was not the first white man to see it, however—trappers had named it years earlier.

Confluence of the Missouri and Yellowstone Rivers, Fort Buford, Montana

April 25, 1805, Thursday

I ascended the hills from where I had a most pleasing view of the country, particularly of the wide and fertile valleys formed by the Missouri and the Yellowstone Rivers.

— (Lewis)

April 26—May 7, 1805

Game was abundant now, so the expedition members did not want for food. Lewis noted, "We can scarcely cast our eyes in any direction without perceiving elk, buffalo, or antelopes." It was on this stretch that the explorers spotted the first bighorn sheep.

Lewis had his first encounter with a grizzly. He eventually killed it, but only after the bear, wounded from Lewis's first shots, had pursued him for some time. A few days later, Lewis, in company with another man, shot ten balls into another grizzly before they killed it.

May 4, 1805, Saturday

The country on both sides of the Missouri continues to be open, level, fertile and beautiful as far as the eye can reach.

(Lewis)

Missouri River near Culbertson, Montana

May 8—19, 1805

On May 8, the expedition came to the river they named the Milk because of the whiteness of its water. They explored it for three miles upriver.

After an uneventful few days, the explorers encountered another grizzly. Six men, all good hunters, went after the bear. Four of them fired at it, each shot wounding the animal. Enraged, the bear charged before the four could reload. The two men who had not fired before then shot at the bear and hit it, but that didn't stop it. The men fled and took refuge in the brush along the riverbank. They reloaded and fired again at the bear, striking it several more times, but this only enraged it further. The bear routed out two of the men, who then ran and jumped into the river off a twenty-foot-high bluff. The bear plunged in after them. Only a few feet from one of the men, the bear was finally killed by a shot from a man on the shore.

While those men were dealing with the bear, a sudden squall struck, upsetting a pirogue that was under sail. Although the boat righted itself, it had filled with water, and most of the cargo, which included the party's scientific instruments, was soaked. During the ensuing two-day layover, the crew managed to dry most of the wet cargo. Nearly all of it, including the instruments, was preserved.

The landscape changed as the party continued upriver. The plains were gradually displaced by rugged hills. Farther west, the hills were covered with pine trees and junipers, which Clark erroneously called cedars. The once broad river was now narrower and more crooked, and the current was swifter. The water was not as muddy as it had been. Springs were almost nonexistent, and side channels were usually dry. Clark dubbed the region the Deserts of America, noting that he doubted it could ever be settled.

Mouth of the Milk River, east of Fort Peck, Montana

May 8, 1805, Wednesday

The water of this river possesses a peculiar whiteness, being about the color of a cup of tea with the admixture of a tablespoonful of milk. From the color of its water we called it Milk River.

(Lewis)

May 20–29, 1805

On May 20, the expedition came to the Musselshell River, so called by the Indians because of the many mollusk shells in the vicinity. By Clark's reckoning, which was remarkably accurate, they were 2,270 miles from the mouth of the Missouri.

A few days after passing the Musselshell, Lewis hiked to the highest point in the vicinity and beheld what he thought were the snowy peaks of the long-sought Rocky Mountains. He wrote, "While I viewed these mountains I felt a secret pleasure in finding myself so near the head of the heretofore conceived boundless Missouri." Lewis had no way of knowing that the formation he saw was probably the Little Rocky Mountains, as

May 23, 1805, Thursday

The country high and broken . . . the tops of the hills covered with scattering pine, spruce and dwarf cedar.

——————— (Lewis)

they are now called—a range many miles east of the Rockies.

Six days later the explorers came to a large, clear river emptying into the Missouri from the south. Clark named it the Judith in honor of Julia (Judy) Hancock of Virginia, who later became his wife.

Missouri River east of Winifred, Montana

Judith River near its mouth, northwest of Winifred, Montana

May 29, 1805, Wednesday

The water of this river is clearer much than any we have met. . . . Captain Clark . . . has thought proper to call it Judith's River.

(Lewis)

May 30—June 2, 1805

The expedition now entered the Breaks of the Missouri, one of the most spectacular areas of the entire trip. The going was so rough and miserable, however, that it surely detracted from the men's appreciation of its beauty. It rained heavily, and a strong head wind blew. Those manning the towropes had to deal with slippery footing in mud—when they could walk on shore at all. Otherwise they pulled the boats while walking through icy water, often chest deep, trying to keep clear of the sharp rocks under the water.

In spite of the difficulties, Lewis recorded at length his impressions of the area's white sandstone bluffs, higher and more sculpted than any they had yet seen. "The water descending . . . has trickled down the soft sand cliffs and worn it into a thousand grotesque figures, which with the help of a little imagination . . . are made to represent elegant ranges of lofty freestone buildings, having their parapets well stocked with statuary."

Eye of the Needle formation [recently destroyed by vandals], White Cliffs of the Missouri River, southeast of Virgelle, Montana

48

White Cliffs of the Missouri River, southeast of Virgelle, Montana

May 31, 1805, Friday

The hills and river cliffs which we passed today exhibit a most romantic appearance. The bluffs of the river rise to the height of from 200 to 300 feet and in most places nearly perpendicular, they are formed of remarkable white sandstone. . . .

(Lewis)

June 3—12, 1805

Leaving the breaks, the Corps came to a "considerable river" entering from the north, and a dilemma presented itself: Which river was the Missouri? The Indians at Fort Mandan had not mentioned the existence of this fork.

Clark explored the southern fork while Lewis explored the northern. After traveling upriver for two days, Clark believed that the southern fork was the Missouri. Lewis, after investigating the northern fork, came to the same conclusion: "Being fully of opinion that [the northern fork] was neither the main stream nor that which it would be advisable for us to take, I determined to give it a name and . . . called it Maria's River," in honor of his cousin Maria Wood.

Just to be sure they had made the right choice, the explorers decided that Lewis and a small party should go ahead overland until they reached either the great falls the Indians at Fort Mandan had described or the "snowy mountains."

June 3, 1805, Monday
This morning early we passed over and formed a camp on the point formed by the junction of these two large rivers. An interesting question was now to be determined; which of these rivers was the Missouri? . . .
— (Lewis)

50

Confluence of the Missouri and Marias Rivers, Loma, Montana

June 13—15, 1805

On June 13, Lewis's "ears were saluted with the agreeable sound of a fall of water . . . which soon began to make a roaring too tremendous to be mistaken for any cause short of the great falls of the Missouri." After Lewis sent a messenger back, Clark and the remaining members of the party moved up and joined Lewis near the falls.

June 13, 1805, Thursday

. . . the grandest sight I ever beheld. . . . The rocks below receive the water in its passage down and breaks it into a perfect white foam which assumes a thousand forms in a moment. . . .

(Lewis)

Rainbow Falls, Great Falls, Montana

June 16—July 14, 1805

Instead of finding a single cascade that could be portaged in a day or so, the explorers were confronted with five falls over a ten-mile stretch of the river. This would mean a portage of considerable length in miles—just over eighteen, as it turned out—and in time.

Because most of this stretch would be impossible to navigate, the Corps had to stop to construct wheeled platforms on which to carry their boats and to place stakes to mark the route of the portage. Along with that, there were delays caused by bad weather—sudden and frequent rain squalls, hail, and gale-force winds—and time spent repairing the resulting damage to equipment. Further slowing down the crew were their sore feet caused by stepping on the abundant prickly-pear cactus, even with their double-soled moccasins.

It was a month before they were again able to put their boats into navigable water. During this time, Clark discovered the Giant Springs, on the Missouri just east of the Great Falls.

June 18, 1805, Tuesday

We proceeded on up the river a little more than a mile to the largest fountain or spring I ever saw. . . . This water . . . is immensely clear and of a bluish cast.

(Clark)

Giant Spring, Giant Springs Heritage State Park, Great Falls, Montana

July 15—19, 1805

The portage accomplished, four days of uneventful travel brought the expedition to what Lewis called the Gates of the Rocky Mountains, a section in which the river is flanked by high rock walls, rising "from the water's edge on either side perpendicularly to the height of 1,200 feet." Lewis commented that the river "seems to have forced its way through this immense body of solid rock for the distance of five-and-three-quarters miles."

July 16, 1805, Tuesday

The river is not so wide as below . . . crowded with islands and crooked.

———————— (Clark)

Missouri River above Great Falls, Montana

Missouri River at Gates of the Mountains, north of Helena, Montana

July 19, 1805, Friday

This evening we entered the most remarkable cliffs that we have yet seen. The towering and projecting rocks in many places seem ready to tumble on us. . . . Nor is there . . . a spot except one of a few yards in extent on which a man could rest the sole of his foot.

(Lewis)

July 20—29, 1805

On July 23, continuing the practice often used before, Clark proceeded on the river while Lewis went overland to explore. Soon Clark's party, which included Sacagawea, entered a section where the river was divided into many channels by numerous large and small islands. Sacagawea recognized the country as the area where her Shoshoni relatives lived. She said that they were close to where the river branched into three forks, and she pointed out the place where she had been captured by the Minitari five years earlier.

Clark reached the forks two days later, again faced with the critical decision about which fork to take. Noticing the greater flow of one fork and that it appeared to emanate from the western mountains, Clark decided it was the "one best calculated for us to ascend." Clark explored a portion of the fork and returned to camp on July 27, where he found Lewis's party waiting for him.

Lewis and Clark both agreed that no one fork was sizable enough to be called the Missouri, so they named the southwest fork, the one they intended to ascend, the Jefferson River. They named the middle fork in honor of secretary of state James Madison, and the eastern fork

Madison River, Three Forks State Park,
Three Forks, Montana

after the secretary of the treasury, Albert Gallatin.

From the time they had left Fort Mandan, the explorers had expected to encounter Indians from the Blackfeet and other western tribes. All along the way, they'd seen evidence of Indian activity— a large recently vacated encampment site, trails, smoke signals—yet no Indians had appeared.

By the time they reached the three forks, Lewis and Clark were especially eager to meet Sacagawea's people. Knowing that soon the river would no longer be navigable, they hoped to secure some horses from the Shoshoni. Horses would be crucial in the overland trek they'd have to take to reach the navigable streams of the Columbia River watershed.

July 25, 1805, Thursday

A fine morning. We proceeded on a few miles to the three forks of the Missouri.

(Clark)

Jefferson and Madison Rivers, Three Forks State Park, Three Forks, Montana

July 30—August 10, 1805

The expedition proceeded onward, Clark's group by water and Lewis's by land. Lewis and his men were walking ahead of the boats, scouting for Indians. They saw some abandoned dwellings but no people. Clark, meanwhile, followed some tracks he assumed had been made by an Indian, but they led only to the top of a hill and disappeared.

Clark began to have problems with the boats in the ever-narrowing, rock-strewn river. In spots, the water was so shallow that the boats had to be carried.

Lewis arrived at a large rock formation and made camp to wait for Clark. While waiting, he explored an Indian trail, again without turning up any Indians.

Sacagawea, who was with Clark's party, spied the rock formation in the distance, recognizing it as one called Beaverhead Rock. She said the rock was not far from her tribe's summer retreat—on a river just over the mountains to the southwest.

After Clark arrived at Lewis's camp, the captains considered their options. Because of the condition of the river, which had narrowed to a stream, Lewis decided that the boats had come to the end of their usefulness.

August 10, 1805, Saturday

Immediately in the level plain stands a high rocky mountain, the base of which is surrounded by the level plain; it has a singular appearance.

(Lewis)

Beaverhead Rock near Dillon, Montana

August 11, 1805

At last Lewis sighted an Indian. Traveling ahead with a small party, he first glimpsed the mounted tribesman through a spyglass. Lewis laid down his gun, and with gifts in his hand slowly advanced. He signaled his men to stay back, but one of them kept moving on. The Indian, no doubt suspicious of a trap, turned his horse and galloped away. The party tried to follow him until a heavy shower erased his horse's tracks.

Trail Creek, Missouri River source,
Sacagawea Memorial Park, Montana

August 12, 1805

After the disappointment of losing sight of the Indian, Lewis and his men set off the next day and headed west over the mountains, the direction the Indian had gone, hoping to find a road that would take them to the Indian village. A few miles along, they passed some abandoned conical huts made of willow. Farther on, they followed a stream that led, as Lewis put it, to "the most distant fountain of the water of the mighty Missouri in search of which we have spent so many toilsome days and restless nights."

The explorers moved on a short distance, and at the top of a ridge they beheld an enormous mountain range. Its towering, snow-covered peaks lined the western horizon as far as the eye could

August 12, 1805,
Monday

This pure and ice cold water . . . issues from the base of a low hill.

(Lewis)

August 12, 1805, Monday ————————————

We proceeded on to the top of the dividing ridge from which I discovered immense ranges of high mountains still to the West of us with their tops partially covered with snow.

(Lewis)

Lemhi Pass, Montana-Idaho border

August 12, 1805,
Monday
. . . *a handsome bold running creek of cold clear water. Here I first tasted the water of the great Columbia River.*

————— (*Lewis*)

*Horseshoe Creek,
Columbia River source,
west side of
Lemhi Pass, Idaho*

see—a sight Lewis was not prepared for. He must have been distressed; after all they had been through, they still had to face crossing this massive obstacle.

After crossing the ridge, the party descended about three-quarters of a mile and came to another creek, this one flowing west—the opposite direction of the stream they had been following on the other side of the ridge. Thus they knew they'd come to one of the headwaters of the Columbia River.

August 13—29, 1805

About ten miles west of the ridge, Lewis sighted three Indians—who he correctly assumed were Shoshoni—on a hill, but as the explorers neared them they disappeared over the crest. Shortly afterward they came upon three Shoshoni women, one of whom ran away. The other two sat down on the ground, as if resigned to their fate. Lewis convinced them that he was friendly, presenting them with gifts. He managed to communicate that he and his men wished to be taken to their village, and the women agreed to lead them.

Along the way, about sixty Shoshoni warriors rode up. When the women showed their chief the presents they had received, the chief dismounted and embraced Lewis. After stopping to smoke the pipe that Lewis proffered, the Indians led the explorers to their village. There Lewis and his men smoked again with the chief, whose name was Cameahwait, and they were given something to eat.

One of Lewis's men was able to communicate in sign language. During the two days at the village, he explained to the chief the purpose of the Corps of Discovery and that the explorers needed horses to take them west over the mountains. He also communicated that Lewis wanted the chief to accompany him back over the ridge and beyond to meet with Clark and the remainder of their party, which included a woman of his nation. The chief agreed.

Three days later, in the early morning, Sacagawea, walking ahead of Clark's party with her husband, saw some Indians in the distance. They were the Shoshoni accompanying Lewis and his men. She began to dance joyously and suck her fingers—a sign indicating that they were her people. Shortly she was recognized by some of the women and they ran to embrace her.

After the party had made camp later that day, Lewis and Clark, ready to hold a council with Cameahwait, sent for Sacagawea to act as interpreter. She entered the tent, sat down, and, after beginning her translation, recognized the chief as her brother. She leaped up and threw her arms around him. After some conversing between the two, she resumed the interpreting, but it was interrupted often by happy tears.

The campsite was dubbed "Camp Fortunate." The majority of the Corps would remain there eight days, gathering information from the Shoshoni about the lands, the waterways, and the tribes to the west—the Flathead and the Nez Perce.

Beaverhead River near Camp Fortunate, south of Dillon, Montana

Meanwhile, Clark took a small party, including some Shoshoni, to reconnoiter a sizable river that lay to the west (the present-day Salmon River). Clark wanted to ascertain whether the river was navigable, even though the Indians had told him it was not. While Clark was away, Lewis was busy bartering for horses with the Shoshoni. He also cached some supplies and sank the pirogues in a pond to conceal them, hoping to retrieve them on the return trip.

On August 25, Lewis and the rest of the Corps, accompanied by the Shoshoni, made their way back to the village to wait for Clark's party to return. There he met the messenger Clark had dispatched to let him know the Indians were right: The river was not a passage to the Pacific Ocean.

Clark rejoined Lewis at the village on August 29.

August 17, 1805, Sunday

We now formed our camp just below the junction of the forks on the larboard side in a level smooth bottom covered with a fine turf of greensward.

(Lewis)

September 9, 1805, Monday ——————————————————

The country in the valley of this river is generally a prairie and from five to six miles wide. . . . The [river] banks are low and its bed entirely gravel.

(Lewis)

August 30—September 9, 1805

The Shoshoni had told Lewis and Clark of a trail through the mountains used by the Nez Perce, and the captains decided that it would be the only feasible way west. So on August 30, with twenty-nine horses and one mule, the Corps, including Sacagawea and her family, headed north toward the trail. On the way they had to cross a high, snowy pass before descending into a valley. Lewis named the river running through it the Clark (the present-day Bitterroot River).

They came upon a sizable village of Flathead, who had never seen white men, and made camp on a small creek nearby. After a friendly visit with the Flathead, during which the captains put their bartering skills to work, the Corps set off with ten new horses.

September 9, 1805, Monday ——————————————————

I determined to halt the next day, rest our horses and take some celestial observations. We called this creek Travelers' Rest.

(Lewis)

*Bitterroot
Valley,
western
Montana*

*Lolo [Travelers
Rest] Creek,
Lolo, Montana*

September 10–13, 1805

The next three days of travel were difficult. On September 13, the expedition came to an area with several hot springs, which they stopped to investigate. After proceeding through more rough country, they camped in a broad open meadow.

September 13, 1805, Friday

I found this water nearly boiling hot at the places it spouted from the rocks.

———— (Clark)

Lolo Hot Springs area, west of Lolo, Montana

Packer Meadow near Lolo Pass, Montana-Idaho border

September 13, 1805, Friday

We proceeded down this creek . . . crossing the creek several times and encamped.

(Clark)

September 14–19, 1805

The terrain now was the worst they had experienced. At altitudes of 7,000 feet and higher, the trail zigzagged sharply in order to ascend the extremely steep slopes, and it was littered with fallen timber. To add to their woes, the weather was miserable—cold and snowing. Clark wrote: "I have been wet and as cold in every part as I ever was in my life." The men were soon exhausted and became so hungry they resorted to eating two of their horses.

Bitterroot Mountains from
Lolo Trail, west of Lolo, Montana

September 15, 1805, Sunday

From this mountain I could observe high rugged mountains in every direction as far as I could see.

— (Clark)

*September 15, 1805,
Sunday*

Here the road . . .
ascends a mountain
winding in every
direction to get
up the steep
ascents. . . .
———— (Clark)

*Lolo Trail, west
of Lolo, Montana*

September 20—29, 1805

The ruggedness of the country eased somewhat and finally the explorers left it behind when they reached Weippe Prairie. Here they met the hospitable Nez Perce, who supplied the explorers with dried salmon and flour made from camas root. During the time spent with the Nez Perce, Lewis and Clark learned of a river suitable for boat travel not far away.

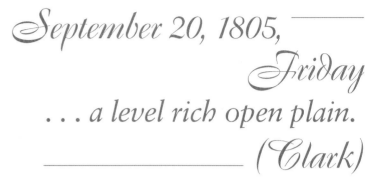

September 20, 1805, Friday

. . . a level rich open plain.

(Clark)

Weippe Prairie, Weippe, Idaho

74

Canoe, Nez Perce National Historical Park, Orofino, Idaho

October 5, 1805, Saturday

Finished and launched two of our canoes this evening which proved to be very good.

(Clark)

September 30—October 5, 1805

After moving a few miles downstream on the river, the Clearwater, the explorers established a camp and commenced building dugout canoes. When they were finished, they set off. Finally, after all these many months, they had a favorable current. They left their horses in the care of the Nez Perce, who agreed to take care of them until their return.

*Snake River near confluence with
Clearwater River, Clarkston, Washington*

*October 10, 1805,
Thursday*
Worthy of remark
that not one stick
of timber on the
river . . .
———— (Clark)

October 6—10, 1805

At first the riverbanks along the explorers' route were covered with tall pines, but as the party went farther downstream the timber thinned, until there was virtually none at all by the time they reached the Clearwater's confluence with the Snake River. Clark described the rivers: "The water of the south fork [Snake] is a greenish blue, the north [Clearwater] as clear as crystal."

October 11–15, 1805

The expedition was now well into the lava lands formed by ancient volcanoes, as arid as the high plains they had traversed earlier in the year. The Snake River coursed through wide canyons formed by low bluffs, some with the volcanic rock exposed, others entirely grass-covered. Rapids, projecting rocks, and windy weather hampered navigation.

October 11, 1805, Friday

Here the country ascends . . . to the high plains and the river is 400 yards wide.

— (Clark)

Snake River, central Washington

Snake River near confluence with Palouse River, Lyons Ferry, Washington

October 13, 1805, Sunday
[a] little river in a . . . bend.
————————— (Clark)

Food was plentiful, as the river teemed with salmon. They ate so much fish, however, that they longed for something different to eat. On October 14, Clark deemed it important enough to note: "For the first time for three weeks past I had a good dinner of blue-wing teal." All along the river they encountered friendly Flathead and Nez Perce Indians, whose primary occupation was fishing.

October 16—18, 1805

When the expedition reached the confluence of the Snake and the Columbia Rivers, it was rather anticlimactic. After all, many weeks before and hundreds of miles back they had tasted the Columbia's waters, and now, having left the canyons of the Snake, the landscape was unremarkable.

October 16, 1805, Wednesday

In every direction from the junction of those rivers the country is one continued plain. . . .

——————— (Clark)

Confluence of the Snake and Columbia Rivers, Pasco, Washington

Hat Rock,
McNary,
Oregon

October 19–22, 1805

After remaining three days at the mouth of the Snake, the expedition set off down the mighty Columbia. The explorers passed many columnar lava formations and caught their first glimpse of a snow-covered peak in the Cascade range.

October 19, 1805, Saturday
. . . a rock . . . resembling
a hat.

——————— (Clark)

October 30, 1805
Wednesday

Saw four cascades caused by small streams falling from the mountains. . . .
— *(Clark)*

October 23–30, 1805

The mountains on the left side of the river became ever higher, and the landscape gradually changed from tawny grasses to green forests of conifers towering above mossy banks. The Corps encountered "swelling and boiling" rapids and waterfalls dropping from great heights. It took the explorers more than a week to cover a mere fifty-five miles, sometimes running the rapids, sometimes portaging around them. In some instances the men had to unload the canoes, portage the cargo, and lower the empty canoes back into the water with ropes they had made of elk hide.

Multnomah Falls, Columbia Gorge, Oregon

October 31, 1805, Thursday

A remarkable high detached rock stands . . . about 800 feet high and 400 paces around, we call the Beacon Rock.

— (Clark)

October 31, 1805

Clark scouted ahead to inspect the next rapid, and he noted that beyond it the river "had every appearance of being affected by the tide." Although this point was more than 100 miles from the sea, he was correct. He also noted an extraordinary, isolated volcanic rock just off the north bank of the river.

Beacon Rock, Columbia River

November 1–4, 1805

Again portaging the cargo and the small canoes, the men maneuvered the four large canoes through what Clark called "the great chute" by "slipping them over the rocks on poles placed across from one rock to another." After another, lesser rapid, the river became wider and more placid, giving the explorers a better opportunity to view the high volcanic peak to the north.

November 2, 1805, Saturday

Here the river widens to near a mile, and the bottoms are more extensive and thickly timbered. . . .

— (Clark)

Columbia River

Mount Adams, Washington

November 4, 1805, Monday ——————————

. . . covered with snow, it rises something in the form of a sugar loaf.

—————————————————— *(Clark)*

November 5—19, 1805

As is typical of the fall climate west of the Cascades, if it wasn't raining it was cloudy, and on many days the fog was so thick that the Corps could not see the opposite shore of the river. On November 7, Clark thought he had his first glimpse of the Pacific Ocean: "Ocean in view. O! the joy." Being nearly twenty miles upriver from the sea, however, he could not have seen it from there. He was looking at the broad and featureless Columbia estuary.

In addition to the rain, the explorers now had to deal with heavy winds, which caused waves so high they could not go on. They had to find campsites on the rocky, inhospitable shore that were above the high-tide line.

Cold and wet, the expedition pushed on when they could. At last, camping on some high ground, Clark wrote on November 15, "The ocean is immediately in front and gives us an extensive view of it from Cape Disappointment to Point Adams." They were 4,133 miles from where they had started out more than a year and a half earlier.

Lewis, who had been traveling by land with a number of others, had already reached the ocean, and returning to Clark's camp on November 17, he reported what he had seen. Because the Corps' dugout canoes could not navigate the rough waters to the sea, Clark took another party overland, where they too stood on the shore and viewed the vastness of the Pacific.

November 19, 1805, Tuesday

I proceeded on the sandy coast and marked my name on a small pine, the day of the month and year. . . .

(Clark)

Pacific Ocean near Cape Disappointment, Washington

Chapter 5
Winter on the Pacific Coast

By the time the Corps of Discovery reached the Pacific Ocean, it was too late in the year to commence the return journey, so they had no choice but to camp for the winter. Clark's camp on the north side of the Columbia would not do because it was exposed to storms and game was scarce. Conditions were better on the south side of the river, according to the Clatsop Indians living there. After thorough exploration, they found a suitable site. It was on a rise of land thirty feet above the high-water line, three miles up a small tributary of the Columbia, about seven miles from the coast.

The shelter they constructed was a square fort measuring fifty feet on each side, with a row of rooms along two facing sides and a parade ground in the middle. A palisade formed both the rear wall and the gated front wall. They named the encampment Fort Clatsop in honor of the local Indians.

By Christmas the fort was nearly complete, and the Corps held a celebration that included exchanging gifts. The day, like most of those preceding it, was, according to Clark, "showery wet and disagreeable." More of the same was in store. Although the temperatures were

*Fort Clatsop National
Memorial, Astoria, Oregon*

*Fort Clatsop National
Memorial, Astoria, Oregon*

moderate, the rainfall was not. From November 4 until March 24, only twelve days were without rain, and six of those were cloudy.

By the time the explorers had arrived at the Pacific, their supply of salt was nearly gone. They needed salt not only to make their food more palatable, but more important, to preserve meat on the return trip, so during the winter the captains ordered some of the men to establish a salt-making operation on the coast.

Lewis and Clark spent much of the time working on their journals and maps and making plans for the return journey. The fort was often visited by Indians of the area—Clatsops, Chinooks, and Cathlamets—who usually brought food and furs to trade.

All winter, Lewis and Clark had hoped to encounter a trade ship from which they could obtain supplies and replenish their trade goods, but none was ever sighted. They'd have to live off the land on the way home.

Pacific Ocean, Seaside, Oregon

Chapter 6
The Return Journey

The Corps of Discovery's return journey began on March 23, 1806, when they launched their flotilla of three dugouts and two canoes on the Columbia River.

About fifty miles upriver, Lewis took the time to explore a few miles of a river the Indians called the Multnomah (now the Willamette). Because its mouth is concealed by many islands, the river had been overlooked the previous fall. From their camp on the Multnomah, the explorers could see three of the Cascade range's most spectacular peaks (named earlier by English explorer George Vancouver): to the north, Mount Rainier and Mount St. Helens, and to the south, Mount Hood.

After a rough passage up the Columbia River, now swollen with spring runoff, the expedition went inland at the Walla Walla River, just a few miles south of the Columbia's confluence with the Snake. They cut across easily traversable plains and arrived at the Snake about seven miles below where it joins the Clearwater. This overland shortcut, a route outlined to them by a Walla Walla chief who had visited their camp, saved them eighty miles.

Now the explorers were back in the country of the friendly Nez Perce. They shortly arrived at the place on the Clearwater where they had left their horses seven months before. At that time Lewis

Mount Hood, northwestern Oregon

and Clark had learned from the Nez Perce chiefs that some of their tribe intended to leave Weippe Prairie in the spring and cross the Bitterroot Mountains. The explorers planned to return in time to accompany them. With that in mind, they had pushed on from Fort Clatsop as quickly as conditions allowed. Now they were disheartened to learn that, because of the deep snow still in the mountains, the Nez Perce wouldn't be leaving for another several weeks.

After waiting about six weeks with the Nez Perce, Lewis and Clark were anxious to get moving, so on June 13 the expedition set off into the Bitterroots without guides. By June 17, after forging through the eight- to ten-foot snowpack and with the trail becoming increasingly hard to see, the Corps turned around and arrived back

Yellowstone River, Billings, Montana

at Weippe Prairie on June 21. Three days later, now with guides they had recruited, the explorers again tackled the trail. This time they made it through.

After covering 156 miles in six days, the group reached the hot springs they'd seen the previous fall. They gratefully basked in the soothing waters before proceeding to Travelers Rest Creek the next day.

While at Fort Clatsop Lewis and Clark had agreed that they would split up at Travelers Rest. Lewis would explore the Marias River more thoroughly while Clark explored the Yellowstone River. They planned to meet later at the mouth of the Yellowstone. On July 3, the two parties went their separate ways.

Clark and his party of twenty-two, including Charbonneau, Sacagawea, and their child, crossed the Continental Divide at what is now called Gibbon Pass, which was farther north than the one the expedition had used the previous year. They followed a route on the east side of the Beaverhead Mountains to Camp Fortunate, where they collected the supplies they had cached and retrieved the boats from the pond. Then they followed the Beaverhead and the Jefferson Rivers to the Three Forks, where Clark sent a detachment of

Pompeys Pillar, east of Billings, Montana

Lewis and Clark Pass near Lincoln, Montana

ten men to the Great Falls for a rendezvous with a contingent from Lewis's party.

A short overland passage from the Three Forks brought Clark and his party to the Yellowstone River. After two days in the boats, they went ashore to examine an unusual sandstone formation rising about 200 feet above the otherwise featureless prairie. Clark named it Pompy's Tower, after Sacagawea's son, whom he had nicknamed Pomp.

Clark reached the mouth of the Yellowstone on August 3. Finding no indication that Lewis and his party had arrived at that point, Clark left a note for Lewis and proceeded on down the Missouri River.

Meanwhile, from Travelers Rest, Lewis headed first east, then after crossing the Continental Divide, northeast, following an overland route to the Missouri. He had learned of the shortcut from the Shoshoni the year before. It took just eight days for Lewis and his party to reach the Missouri River a few miles from the Great Falls. The previous year, the expedition had spent two months traveling from that point to Travelers Rest.

Lewis took only three men with him to explore the Marias. He left the other six men at the Great Falls with orders to

Missouri River near Mobridge, South Dakota

wait for Clark's detachment. Afterward they were to again portage the canoes and supplies around the falls and meet Lewis at the mouth of the Marias.

Lewis and his small party set off overland to a place on the Marias upriver of his original stopping point. They proceeded up the river to where it branched, then followed the northern branch. Traveling west, eventually Lewis could see that the river issued from the Rocky Mountains. Having found the source of the Marias, he needed to explore no further.

On the way downriver, Lewis and his three men encountered eight Blackfeet Indians. They appeared to be friendly, so Lewis invited them to camp with him and his men overnight. At dawn, the Blackfeet made a move to take the explorers' guns and horses. A scuffle ensued, during which two of the Blackfeet were killed. The others took refuge in a nearby gulch. Presuming there were other Blackfeet nearby and fearing retaliation, Lewis ordered his men to pack up for a quick departure.

In just over twenty-four hours, with only occasional stops to rest, the party covered 120 miles. They reached the Missouri well to the west of the mouth of the Marias, and there, Lewis wrote, they "had the unspeakable satisfaction of seeing our canoes coming down." The four exhausted men hastily unloaded their horses, turned them loose, and clambered aboard the boats, wasting no time in resuming the voyage. They didn't know whether the Blackfeet were pursuing them, but they saw no more of them.

On August 7, Lewis and his party reached the mouth of the Yellowstone. Finding Clark's note, they moved on downriver. The two contingents of the Corps were reunited on August 12.

Six weeks later, on September 23, 1806, after a swift and uneventful trip down the Missouri, the Corps of Discovery arrived at Camp Wood, the point from which they had departed. They had been gone for two years, four months, and ten days and had covered over 8,000 miles.

The epic journey of Lewis and Clark was remarkable for more than its scope. It was accomplished with no discord between its captains, little misconduct among the men, and—other than the death of Sergeant Floyd, which would undoubtedly have occurred in any case—no loss of life, severe injuries, or serious illnesses.

Although Lewis and Clark did not find a navigable water route to the Pacific Ocean, as Jefferson had hoped they would, their contributions to the expansion of the West were enormous. They mapped many of the lands and waterways of the Northwest, established good relations with most of the Indian tribes they encountered, and provided a wealth of material on the previously unknown flora and fauna of the territory.

The final cost of the expedition was $38,722.25. While the figure was far higher than Lewis's original estimate, Jefferson and the nation received full value for the investment.

Gateway Arch, Jefferson National Expansion Memorial, St. Louis, Missouri

Bibliography

Appleman, Roy E. *Lewis and Clark: Historic Places Associated with Their Transcontinental Exploration (1804–06)*. Edited by Robert G. Ferris. Reprint. St. Louis: The Lewis & Clark Trail Heritage Foundation, Jefferson National Expansion Historical Association, 1993.

Biddle, Nicholas, ed. *The Journals of the Expedition of Lewis and Clark*. New York: Heritage Press, 1962.

Chidsey, Donald Barr. *Lewis and Clark: The Great Adventure*. New York: Crown Publishers, 1970.

De Voto, Bernard. *The Journals of Lewis and Clark*. Boston: Houghton Mifflin Company, 1953.

Fanselow, Julie. *The Traveler's Guide to the Lewis & Clark Trail*. Helena, Mont.: Falcon Press, 1994.

Hawke, David Freeman. *Those Tremendous Mountains: The Story of the Lewis and Clark Expedition*. New York: W. W. Norton & Co., 1980.

Lavender, David. *The Way to the Western Sea: Lewis and Clark Across the Continent*. New York: Doubleday, Anchor Books, 1988.

Moulton, Gary E., ed. *The Journals of the Lewis and Clark Expedition*. 11 vols. Lincoln, Nebr.: University of Nebraska Press, 1986–87.

Thwaites, Reuben Gold, ed. *The Original Journals of the Lewis and Clark Expedition*. 8 vols. New York: Dodd, Mead & Co, 1904–5.

Wheeler, Olin D. *The Trail of Lewis and Clark, 1804–1904*. 2 vols. Reprint. New York: AMS Press, 1976.

List of Illustrations

Index

About the Authors

Husband and wife **Bill and Jan Moeller** are professional photographers and authors. Since 1982 they have traveled full-time in their RV to photograph historical sites around the United States. Having their home with them allows the Moellers to stay in an area as long as necessary to take pictures and do research for their unique photographic history books, of which *Lewis and Clark: A Photographic Journey* is the fifth.

Before embarking on their land-based ventures, the Moellers lived aboard a sailboat for twelve years. In addition to their photo histories, the authors have published two successful volumes on sailing and three on RV travel, as well as writing a syndicated newspaper column called "RV Traveling." The Moellers' previous full-color history titles include the popular *Chief Joseph and the Nez Perces: A Photographic History*, published by Mountain Press in 1995.

Other books by Bill and Jan Moeller:

Chief Joseph and the Nez Perces:
  A Photographic History

A Complete Guide to Full-time RVing:
  Life on the Open Road

Crazy Horse, His Life, His Lands:
  A Photographic Biography

Custer, His Life, His Adventures:
  A Photographic Biography

The Intracoastal Waterway:
  A Cockpit Cruising Handbook

Living Aboard:
  The Cruising Sailboat as a Home

The Oregon Trail:
  A Photographic Journey

RV Electrical Systems

RVing Basics

We encourage you to patronize your local bookstore. Most stores will order any title that they do not stock. You may also order directly from Mountain Press using the order form provided below or by calling our toll-free number and using your MasterCard or VISA. We will gladly send you a complete catalog upon request.

Some other titles of interest:

_____Lewis & Clark: *A Photographic Journey* $18.00/paper

_____The Journals of Patrick Gass:
        Member ofthe Lewis and Clark Expedition $20.00/paper $36.00/cloth

_____Chief Joseph and the Nez Perces:
        A Photographic Journey $15.00/paper

_____Lakota Noon:
        The Indian Narrative of Custer's Defeat $18.00/paper $36.00/cloth

_____Children of the Fur Trade:
        Forgotten Métis of the Pacific Northwest $15.00/paper

_____The Piikani Blackfeet: *A Culture Under Siege* $18.00/paper $30.00 cloth

_____William Henry Jackson: *Framing the Frontier* $22.00/paper $36.00 cloth

Please include $3.00 per order to cover shipping and handling.

Send the books marked above. I enclose $ _____

Name _____

Address _____

City/State/Zip _____

☐ Payment enclosed (check or money order in U.S. funds)

Bill my: ☐ VISA   ☐ MasterCard   Expiration Date: _____

Card No. _____

Signature _____

MOUNTAIN PRESS PUBLISHING COMPANY
P.O. Box 2399 • Missoula, MT 59806
Order Toll Free 1-800-234-5308 • Have your VISA or MasterCard ready.
e-mail: mtnpress@montana.com • website: www.mtnpress.com